THE CRYSTAL-CLEAR

LEADER

A Proven System for Maximizing Your Success, Productivity, and Profitability

ERIC JACKIER

PEAK PRESS

An Imprint for GracePoint Publishing (www.GracePointPublishing.com)

GracePoint Matrix, LLC
624 S. Cascade Ave
Suite 201
Colorado Springs, CO 80903
www.GracePointMatrix.com
Email: *Admin@GracePointMatrix.com*
SAN # 991-6032

Library of Congress Control Number: 2021918431

ISBN-13: (Paperback) – 978-1-951694-82-1
eISBN: (eBook) - 978-1-951694-81-4

Books may be purchased for educational, business, or sales promotional use.
For bulk order requests and price schedule contact:
Orders@GracePointPublishing.com

For more great books, please visit GracePoint Publishing
online at www.gracepointpublishing.com

PEAK PRESS

Endorsements

This inspiring, motivational book will help you unlock your leadership abilities. Read it, apply it, and let these ideas change your life!

—Brian Tracy, Author/Speaker/Consultant

This is one of the greatest books you'll ever read. Eric is real, authentic, and most importantly transparent. He brings his experience and the lessons he's learned. He also shares his mistakes which are always the best lessons!

—Patty Aubery
#1 *New York Times* Best-selling Author, *Chicken Soup for the Working Woman's Soul*, Former President Jack Canfield Companies, Founder of Permission Granted and CVO of Goalfriends.org

The Crystal-Clear Leader provides the basis for a leadership and productivity method that is based on well-researched principles that can help you reach your goals and achieve success faster and with greater efficiency. The engaging and conversational style will allow you to relate to the challenges Eric faced during his journey to success. The quizzes at the end of each chapter are excellent tools for self-reflection and implementation for you and your business or organization. I highly recommend Eric's book.

—David Krueger, MD, Founder,
NeuroMentor® Institute for Peak Performance

CONTENTS

Foreword xi

Preface xiii

Introduction xv

Part One

Leadership Foundational Principles

Chapter One 3
    Integrity

Chapter Two 6
    Trust

Chapter Three 9
    Courage

Chapter Four.. 13
    Decision-Making

Chapter Five... 16
    Execution

Chapter Six 20
    Effective Communication

Chapter Seven 25
    The Ability to Listen

Part Two

Leadership Responsibilities

Chapter Eight...31
   Vision

Chapter Nine 34
   Mission

Chapter Ten 37
   Clarity

Chapter Eleven...41
   Goal Setting

Chapter Twelve 44
   Strategic Planning

Chapter Thirteen..49
   Management Responsibilities

Chapter Fourteen 52
   Team-Building

Chapter Fifteen 56
   Staffing

Chapter Sixteen..62
   Delegation

Chapter Seventeen...65
   Time Management

Chapter Eighteen 69
   Crisis Management

Chapter Nineteen..77
   Flexibility

Chapter Twenty 81
   Continuous Improvement

Chapter Twenty-One 85
   Hard Work and Preparation

Conclusion 89

Acknowledgements 91

Eric Jackier's Professional Affiliations and Certifications 93

About the Author 95

FOREWORD

I first met Eric when he took my Train the Trainer course. It quickly became obvious that he had a great deal of tenacity and desire to get ahead and succeed in life. Since that time, he has become an extremely well-qualified and highly regarded coach who has developed several powerful programs on leadership and business development. And now he has written this book that you hold in your hands.

As you read *The Crystal-Clear Leader*, you will notice that Eric talks a great deal about his previous failure as a business owner and how he used what he learned to become a success. This rare transparency from a now-successful leader allows you to not only take the journey from failure to success with him, but it also allows you to deeply examine where you are in your own journey of business and leadership development.

This is not a book to be read and put away on the shelf. It is a book that can and should be read and referred to many times. Each chapter focuses on a specific area of leadership that is critical for success in business and personal development. Make sure to take the time to study and master each one. As you'll discover, Eric sets a standard for excellence in everything he does. In this book he shows you how to do the same.

I have enjoyed getting to know Eric over the years, both personally and professionally, as he is a member of my Success Accelerator Mastermind group. Now you get to enjoy knowing him too. What I love is that his conversational and optimistic approach to life and leadership comes through in *The Crystal-Clear Leader* just as it does when you are with him in person.

Enjoy this book, and let Eric help you achieve the success you are looking for. I promise you will be glad you invested the time to do it!

—Jack Canfield, coauthor of the #1 *New York Times* Best-selling
Chicken Soup for the Soul® series and *The Success Principles™:
How to Get from Where You Are to Where You Want to Be.*

PREFACE

You have something in common with Napoleon, Tom Brady, and Queen Elizabeth I—you are a leader!

The statement above is true. Whether you lead a large corporation, small business, or nothing at all, *you* are the leader of your own life.

As Brian Tracy often says, "Leaders are made, not born." Another great leader, John Maxwell, says, "Everything rises and falls on leadership." These statements are also true. I know this firsthand because I'm living proof! I *thought* I was a leader; I thought I was a good one, too. But as you will learn, I couldn't have been more wrong . . .

The story of my previous failures and how I became the leadership and mentoring coach I am today will be told in depth in the following introduction. In the rest of the book, I will then share the secrets and principles that have helped me become the very best leader I can be—a crystal-clear leader.

INTRODUCTION

My Path to Success: Becoming a Crystal-Clear Leader

I began my career as a sports broadcaster in the era long before the internet came along, which means the two choices for career opportunities were either radio or television. The hard part was that unless you were a professional athlete, your chances of "breaking in" were minimal. After a few years of having some, but not enough, success (the true recurring theme of my personal and professional life), I tried sales, fundraising for nonprofit organizations, and even had a job as the circulation director of a magazine devoted to people with disabilities.

My desire to be my own boss and pave my own way to success led me to begin a company called Enable Enterprises. Enable was my answer to helping people with disabilities with a for-profit model. While the company did make some impressive strides over a twelve-year period in helping people with disabilities in the areas of online education, mentoring, and social security benefits retention, it ultimately failed.

The failure of the business coincided with the failure of my marriage. Unfortunately, the failures of both were intertwined, which caused the complete collapse of my life in just about every way imaginable. Before all was said and done, I had no marriage, no business, and since I was living in an extended-stay hotel, no home. There was also a mountain of debt I couldn't pay, and as I was approaching the age of fifty, I had very little hope for my future. The way I saw it, I was speeding toward a life no one would want for themselves.

I remember that awful, depressing feeling so well—a mixture of anger, depression, and bitterness. For a while, it was overwhelming. It was common for me to sleep all morning, eat, make two or three calls to try and help my situation, then quit for the day. Then I'd simply watch TV, eat dinner, and then watch more TV until bedtime.

It was quite a mess. There were two choices for me at that point—survive or perish! There were still enough people in my life who mattered. My wonderful family and a pet cat who needed me were at the head of the line. I chose to survive, but I also knew drastic changes were necessary.

In order to create the changes needed, I had to deeply examine everything in my life. As I did, I began to realize I'd brought myself to this point. I'm the person who "wrote" this story. I had done this by continuing to repeat certain patterns throughout my adult life:

- Choosing the wrong type of career by always trying to "reinvent the wheel." My ideas were good, but they weren't always practical, and they certainly weren't financially viable or responsible.
- Turning away from some of my natural strengths to achieve those goals.
- Surrounding myself with people who didn't necessarily have my best interests at heart instead of listening to the people who did and trusting my instincts, which had proven to be good in the past. I took way too much bad and destructive advice.
- Allowing my stubbornness to stop me from extricating myself from what I knew were unhappy and unhealthy situations.
- Trying to please other people by tolerating certain situations that were destructive to me and my personal, professional, and financial well-being. This had been a lifetime pattern of mine.

Many of these unpleasant facts were difficult to admit and, in some cases, hard to recognize. As I began to go through this process, I sought professional help. I needed it badly—I recognized that, too! As my doctor helped me through the process of becoming aware, I began to understand that I had to *own* the story I authored for myself.

This wasn't an easy mental place to get to, especially given the fact that I had a lot of outside help in getting to where I was. It was valid and factually correct to place blame on many dishonest people who took advantage of me, including some of the people who were "closest" to me.

Ultimately, though, the responsibility was mine when it came to my situation. I made certain choices when I could have made different ones. I allowed certain situations to develop and continue when I could have stopped them; I chose not to. I own my decisions and mistakes. I and I alone own my story.

As I began to assess my situation, I was thoroughly angry and upset that I had let myself get into this position. I was unrecognizable to myself. It was hard to believe that someone who had the intestinal fortitude to overcome a physical disability and live a normal life could have failed so spectacularly in every area that mattered. It was beyond obvious that complete and major changes needed to be made if I was going to make a comeback and become the successful person I wanted to be and knew I could be. It wasn't too late as long as I was willing to do what was necessary—and I was.

The first step was figuring out what changes I needed to make, and then I would decide where to go from that point. As I took stock of my situation, I began to realize I'd stopped doing many things I'd always enjoyed and been successful at in the past. This included:

- Public speaking
- Mentoring
- Being in a position of leadership

I had no idea at that point what exactly I wanted to do with those things. Just before my wife left, I had mentioned the possibility of exploring these areas as the basis for a new career. She refused to support my efforts and instead told me I needed to stop dreaming and "be like the rest of the world." In her mind, this meant I needed to get up at 6:00 a.m., catch the subway, and get a nine-to-five job. Now that she was gone, I decided to follow my instincts and see what might happen. My other major decision was to formally shut down my old company and exit the profession I had been a part of for twenty years.

I began to explore opportunities that would provide me with specialized training and certify me in the areas of speaking, training, and coaching. The first two courses I enrolled in were fine, but they were not for me. They were too much "do it yourself" and not enough support. I needed something more comprehensive. A few days later, I found the John Maxwell Leadership Certification program. If I completed the program successfully, I would be certified as a speaker and coach with the ability to use John Maxwell's world-famous tools and materials. The courses were six months long and would require a significant financial investment. After careful thought and discussion—and with some trepidation—I went ahead.

I quickly realized that I certainly charted a new course for myself. Completing the Maxwell course required everyday effort on my part. I moved out of the hotel and found a lovely apartment that would also serve as my new office. Having a fresh start in a new home did wonders for me emotionally. The comfortable surroundings allowed me to focus on getting work done.

The culmination of the Maxwell certification was a five-day convention in Orlando, Florida. In order to complete the certification, participants were required to give a table speech that was within thirty seconds of five minutes and twenty-five seconds. As luck would have it, I hit the time exactly on the mark. My peers voted me the best speaker and best potential coach at our table. I later found out that I had scored in the top ten for the entire convention.

That success led to an opportunity that entirely changed my professional life. Through Maxwell, I received an invitation to attend the Brian Tracy Speaking Academy, a three-day course in beautiful San Diego, California, where Mr. Tracy would personally work with each of the participants individually and in group settings. It was an excellent course. Luckily for me, and perhaps due to the fact that Brian had been dealing with some physical issues from a fall he had taken, he took an interest in me. At the end of the three days, he told me: "You can make a living as a speaker, but you still need work. In order to be the best, you need to put in an extra three percent to distinguish yourself from the other ninety-seven percent."

I came home from San Diego and got to work. I studied more of Brian's material (with his blessing), joined his inner circle mastermind group, and sent him recordings of my speeches. Brian very kindly suggested that I work with one of his business coaches. Over time, she completely changed my thinking about what my business could become. She suggested that

I consider adding certified coaching to my professional qualifications, adding my own and other leadership materials in addition to Maxwell. I never thought I could be able to handle so much.

Brian Tracy wasn't done with me. He was proud of the fact I'd worked so hard on what he suggested. He made another introduction for me to the world-famous success coach Jack Canfield. I am proud to say Jack has become my friend and mentor. It was an honor to appear as his guest on his television show *Talking About Success*.

Jack told me about his Success Principles course, and I happily enrolled in it. I passed the course quickly, and that led to another opportunity that fundamentally changed my career. Jack offered me the opportunity to receive his certified coach training. This training evolved over time and became extensive. It takes hundreds and even thousands of hours to become a top-flight coach, but the rewards have been more than worth it. Coaching is a wonderful profession that has given me the opportunity to share what I have learned with so many wonderful people who are looking to become more successful than they ever thought possible.

The advice Brian Tracy and Jack Canfield gave me changed my life and set me on a path that led me to develop the Eric Jackier Leadership System. *The Crystal-Clear Leader* is the direct result of all that I have learned as my system evolved.

What Is a Crystal-Clear Leader?

A crystal-clear leader is a leader who has achieved excellence in twenty-one key areas of leadership. The first seven are foundational principles every leader must have at all times in order to be successful. They are:

- Integrity
- Trust
- Courage
- The ability to decide
- The ability to execute and move forward
- Effective communication skills
- The ability to listen

The next fourteen are also critically important for the leader to make an organization of any kind successful.

- Values
- Mission
- Absolute clarity
- Goal setting
- Hiring and developing key people
- Team building
- Strategic planning
- Crisis anticipation
- Crisis management
- Flexibility
- Problem solving
- Delegation
- Focus
- Foresight

The chapters in this book will discuss each of these leadership areas. I've included questions and exercises to help you improve and develop your leadership skills. I can't make any promises or guarantees, but if you commit to doing the work and avoid taking shortcuts, you will likely improve at a transformational level, and your business, company, or organization will become more successful than it's ever been before.

Are you ready to make it happen?

PART ONE

Leadership Foundational Principles

CHAPTER ONE

Integrity

Let's begin with a good news/bad news scenario. First, the bad news: if you're a leader who has issues with integrity, you're in trouble. Without this key trait, your business or the organization you lead ultimately won't succeed; it certainly won't reach the level of success you hope to achieve. Now for the good news: like almost anything else, you can change course and become a leader who operates with a higher level of integrity than you did before.

Integrity has a lot to do with character. It shows up in the way you conduct yourself as a leader and as a person. It also shows itself in your interactions with your customers and employees. People notice!

I have been around leaders of varying degrees of integrity for many years. I have also (albeit unintentionally) conducted myself in both high and low degrees of integrity. I will say, though, that since I began JTD Coaching and Consulting, I have not conducted myself with anything less than one-hundred percent integrity. How can I say that so confidently? The answer is that I am now extremely conscious of several important points:

- I make one-hundred percent certain that I deliver the *exact* service I promise.
- All agreements are in writing and formally understood before going forward—with anyone.
- Expectations are clearly spelled out between myself, my associates, my vendors, and my clients.
- Deadlines are met, and payments are made on time. If arrangements need to be changed, it's done beforehand so people can manage their own affairs without too much difficulty.

- I do not take shortcuts with the quality of my coaching, my books, or my presentations.
- I will not work with anyone, internally or externally, who doesn't exhibit the same qualities I demand from myself. If I find out I am, I will terminate the relationship as quickly as possible.

A crystal-clear leader operates under these principles. *He or she will not compromise their principles for any short- or long-term gain.*

When leaders operate with integrity, they are shown to be consistent, ethical leaders people will want to follow.

You cannot be a crystal-clear leader if you don't have integrity. It's that simple.

The good news is that every human being can improve their skill level and increase their personal and professional growth. This includes integrity. Please answer the questions below as honestly as possible. If you do, you may be able to identify areas and gaps where you can improve on this core leadership principle.

Questions and Exercises:

1. Name three instances when you may not have acted with the highest level of integrity.

2. What are three to five areas within your business you will not compromise on?

3. Do the people who work with you (vendors, partners, or associates) operate with the highest level of integrity? How about your employees?

4. What, if anything, must you improve within your company or organization in order to operate with the highest level of integrity?

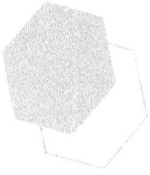

CHAPTER TWO

Trust

You've probably heard this before, but it bears repeating: without trust, there is very little chance of leadership success.

Of all the foundational principles, this is the hardest one of all. We have all violated someone's trust at one time or another. It always causes damage, and this damage can be enormous. When trust is violated, it's essential that immediate corrective action be taken.

As a leader, you must do the following if you have violated the trust of a customer, partner, or employee:

- Admit your mistake.
- Apologize sincerely.
- Do whatever is necessary to fix the situation.
- Ask for forgiveness and a chance to prove it won't happen again.

If you are unable to immediately fix the situation, commit to a plan—in writing, if necessary—that will fix the issue and do whatever it takes to stick to that plan.

Anyone can make a mistake. It happens, and if good faith efforts are made to fix what has been broken, the breach can hopefully be repaired.

A crystal-clear leader is someone people count on. Why? Because they know what they can expect. They feel safe in the knowledge they are working with or for someone who will improve their skill level, sell them a product or service they need, help them build their dreams, and contribute to their upward mobility.

Before I founded my own business, I worked for five different leaders. Three of them were quite successful. Only one of them was a crystal-clear leader. Not a perfect leader (no one is), but certainly a crystal-clear leader. If you were to ask me what set him apart from all the others, it was his trustworthiness.

I wish I could say I was a crystal-clear leader at all times in my business career. I wasn't. I look back now and realize I had some glaring weaknesses that caused a lot of problems. The biggest of these was my inability to deliver unpleasant news when it was necessary. Perhaps even worse, I tended to procrastinate, so I would try and sweep these kinds of situations under the rug for as long as possible. I always figured that somehow, some way, I would be able to stall, buy time, and miraculously, these kinds of situations would work themselves out. This wasn't leadership; it was wishful thinking that caused problems financially and damaged my personal and professional relationships over time. I wish I had the ability to go back and change the way I handled things during those days. Unfortunately, that's impossible. The good news is that I have learned from the mistakes I made. Mistakes, even big ones, can be overcome if you commit to doing things the right way going forward. Shortcuts don't work. Crystal-clear leaders avoid them—and succeed.

Questions and Exercises:

1. Think of a situation in which you violated someone's trust. What did you do to rectify the situation? Did it help?

2. If you could go back and fix a situation in which a lack of trust was created, how would you fix it?

3. Are you a leader people trust? Ask three of your closest associates for their thoughts.

CHAPTER THREE

Courage

Courage can mean many things. It also has many connotations when it comes to leadership. Here are a few examples.

- In my opinion, the amazing foresight and leadership of **George Washington** makes him the only one of our Founding Fathers who could have served as our first president. If you don't believe me, go through some of the biographies of our Founding Fathers and study their thoughts at the Constitutional Convention in 1787. The Founding Fathers themselves collectively had plenty of courage to break away from the British Empire. However, Washington, and only Washington, had the foresight and courage to see well beyond his lifetime and realize that the example he set as president would resonate throughout the history of the new United States. The practices he used to fill his cabinet, the appointment of the original justices to the Supreme Court, his consultations with the newly formed Congress (including the inevitable balancing act that would develop among the three co-equal branches of our government), his insistence on only having two terms (especially since he truly could have served as long as he wanted and turned the presidency into a monarchy)—all of this took enormous courage and personal sacrifice on his part. Thus, what he accomplished has directly impacted our country for over two centuries.
- How about **Abraham Lincoln**? He had the courage to take on the despicable stain on our country known as slavery, something our Founding Fathers ultimately declined to address as a nation. Lincoln realized that as the country expanded, the issue had to be

dealt with once and for all. He also had the courage to take sides. He was willing to do what had to be done to eliminate the awful practice that was tearing our country apart. How many leaders historically have been willing to directly take on an issue that easily could have and would have destroyed the United States? You can easily count them on one hand, before and after Lincoln.

- Let's look at a great leader from the world of sports, the greatest coach who ever lived: **John Wooden**. Born in Indiana into a hardscrabble but loving farm family, he grew up understanding the value of hard work and dedication to learning a craft. He became one of the best basketball players in the state of Indiana. When he got married and realized he might need an alternative to a professional basketball career, he became both an English teacher and the basketball coach at what was then known as Indiana State College. Becoming a widely recognized and highly regarded coach, he received an offer to become the head coach of the University of California, Los Angeles (UCLA). At the time, Southern California was as foreign to him as China. He was really hoping to receive the same offer from the University of Minnesota.

Wooden exhibited two kinds of courage. He risked everything he and his wife knew and loved to take advantage of an opportunity he desperately wanted, even if it was in a place he and his family knew nothing about. It was a huge risk—and an uncomfortable one, at that. He took it, and the rest is history.

The second brand of courage revealed Coach Wooden's character. He actually received the offer from the University of Minnesota two days after he accepted the position at UCLA. It included everything he asked for . . . and a lot more money. He declined the offer he really wanted because he had given his word to UCLA. How many people would have done that?

If you're interested in learning what made John Wooden the greatest coach who ever lived, you can study his world-famous Pyramid of Success by visiting www.jtdcoaching.com. I'm the only coach in the eastern United States who is certified to teach it.

The three leaders we discussed are certainly examples of tremendous courage in leadership. While we may never achieve that sort of immortality in leadership, we can certainly look to achieve crystal-clear leadership when it comes to courage and leading our companies or organizations.

When it comes to courage, a crystal-clear leader:

- Keeps their word and commitments even if it requires sacrificing their personal wishes or desires
- Sees situations within their company as they are—not how they necessarily wish they could be—and reacts accordingly
- Makes fundamental changes within their organization or business for the long-term, even if it's at the expense of the short-term
- Pulls the plug when necessary on projects and personnel

Having the courage to do what might be necessary despite the consequences can be very difficult, as can seeing situations objectively and clearly. I only wish I'd had the courage to look at things as they were with my last company. Had I done so, I would have seen what should have been obvious. My business was not built on a solid foundation, and because of that, there was really no way to achieve long-term success. The industry I was working in at the time really wasn't an "industry" at all. I made the mistake of letting my stubbornness and determination to be successful cloud my judgment. While there are times when stubbornness and determination can be useful and important in overall success, a crystal-clear leader has the key ability to see what will work and what doesn't.

Questions and Exercises:

1. Describe a situation going on within your organization that might require crystal-clear leadership courage to resolve.

2. What are some areas within your organization that may not be as successful as you wish them to be despite your efforts and/or significant investment?

3. If you did not handle a previous situation with the type of courage you needed at the time, what would you do differently now if you could?

4. In order to grow or expand your business or organization in the future, how will you exhibit the courage to make it happen successfully?

CHAPTER FOUR

Decision-Making

This is as clear and simple as it gets: If you can't make decisions, there is no way you can lead. While this is the main takeaway from this chapter, that's not all there is to it. Learning to make good and important decisions is a key leadership skill that can be improved over time. A crystal-clear leader knows something else most leaders are unfamiliar with: they understand the importance of the decision-making process. That's right! There are numerous ways to make successful and important decisions. While no leader is one-hundred percent correct (in fact, studies show that 70 percent of the time, the decisions leaders make will not work out as they hope), a good leader, and especially a crystal-clear leader, knows how to greatly increase their odds of success. The key to increase the odds of success is **knowing and understanding your business.**

The Three Primary Types of Decision-Making:

1. **Command Decisions** – These are decisions made by the leader and only the leader. Command decisions typically are made in the immediacy of the moment and are usually critical and time-sensitive.
2. **Consultation Decisions** – The leader usually makes the final decision with significant input from trusted advisors and others who have significant interests in the company or organization. The decisions are usually key ones with long-term effects.
3. **Collaboration Decisions** – These decisions are made in group settings where everyone has a vote, with the majority winning the

decision. This type of decision-making is usually used in board meetings as well as in many nonprofit organizations.

Each of these decision-making types has advantages and disadvantages. My personal preference is number two. I like feedback and input from my key people. Many times, they may see something or know of a situation that I might not be aware of. I am not a fan of collaboration decisions. Group decisions can easily lead to inaction and polarization. There also are times when command decisions must be made immediately. These are usually reserved for crisis management situations, which we'll tackle in a later chapter.

The crystal-clear decision-making process should include several contributing factors:

- What are we deciding?
- What are we hoping to achieve with this decision?
- When must the decision be made?
- What are the short-, medium-, and long-term ramifications of this decision?
- What happens if we decide to do nothing?
- What are the financial consequences of this decision? Can we afford it? Can we afford not to go forward?
- If it's an external decision, do we have an in-house alternative?
- If we are working with an outside vendor, how do they add value to our company and our bottom line?
- What do we want the end result to be if the decision is successful?
- What are the consequences to the company if the decision made is the wrong one?

Once that information is gathered and analyzed, a decision should be made and executed. We'll talk about executing decisions very shortly.

Questions and Exercises:

1. Which of the three types of decision-making mentioned above most resembles yours?

2. How have your last five major decisions turned out? List the outcomes and the thinking behind them.

3. List the major decisions coming up for your company over the next three to six months. Which of the processes above will you use to execute them?

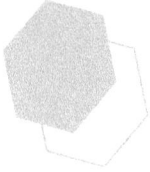

CHAPTER FIVE

Execution

Okay, the decision has been made; what happens next? The leader must make sure the decision is executed. This simply means that what was decided is implemented. The crystal-clear leader does more than that, though; he or she develops an implementation process that increases the odds for a successful outcome.

The crystal-clear leader takes several key steps once a decision is made, keeping in mind that he or she should perform only the parts of the implementation that must be done by the leader. *Only* the leader.

The key to successfully implementing an important decision is to create what I call an *implementation structure.* This is a process I have used successfully for myself and the people I work with. Let me show you how this works. I'll use a recent example based on our customer lead generation strategy.

When my marketing team proposed changing some of our outreach strategies to prospective clients, it made sense. I quickly realized two things. First, I needed it spelled out for me in detail so I would understand how it would work. Second, I could not and should not manage the new strategy myself. Once we decided to go ahead, here's how we implemented the decision.

1. I delegate the oversight of the project to my Chief Operating Officer (COO). While each of the four people involved (including me) had a role in the process, I knew my COO could not only oversee how things were working but could also host weekly calls with the marketing team without me. That would free extra time for me to do the work only I could do for the business. I made it clear that I wanted to be updated weekly on how things were going.

2. The COO and my marketing team held a series of calls and exchanged several emails. Those led to the development of a systematic process we would use with every prospect.
3. The system they came up with accomplished everything I hoped it would. Its successful implementation has done the following for the company:

- It has given us clarity as to who our best prospective customers are.
- It has created a highly organized, three-step screening process to help determine whether the prospect is a candidate who may become a client.
- It has cut down on wasted time for everyone, especially me.
- It has yielded much better prospects than we had before we began our new marketing strategy. This was the goal all along.

Let's now go back and review the process. Here are the steps for executing your strategy once a key decision is made:

1. **Delegation** – The worst thing you can do as a leader is to micromanage everyone and everything. I guarantee you will fail as a leader, and ultimately your company will fail too. I was certain the team I hired knew how to do their jobs, and I also knew my COO could work with them and manage the process so I wouldn't have to.
2. **Team Ownership** – Everyone had direct input into how our new system would be implemented and run. They each had a personal and professional stake in the program's success.
3. **Buy-in** – Because they had ownership in the process and the freedom to design it, they went the extra mile to make sure it was successful. You can't ask for more than that.
4. **Clarity** – Everyone knew their role. They also knew what I wanted the new system to accomplish and what my expectations were. They were familiar with my tendencies when it came to communicating with me. It made everyone's job much easier, and things ran smoothly.

5. **Periodic Review** – We examine our results every thirty days to make sure things are working as they should. We make adjustments and corrections as necessary as a team. You should, too!

Questions and Exercises:

1. Have you been able to execute your decisions successfully over the last six to twelve months? Why or why not?

2. Do you or your company use an implementation structure as you execute your decisions? If so, what are the steps you take?

3. Can your implementation steps and structure be improved? What additional steps can you take to do so?

4. How much input do you give your team on the implementation of key decisions?

5. Describe the way you as a leader communicate how you want decisions executed. Has this been successful?

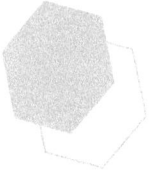

CHAPTER SIX
Effective Communication

Throughout history, most memorable leaders were great communicators. To illustrate this point, let's examine the communication styles and the legacies of two American presidents who served consecutively during the Great Depression. The first was Herbert Hoover, and the second was his successor, Franklin Delano Roosevelt. Many prominent historians have stated that had they served in the reverse order, they would be remembered differently.

Herbert Hoover, the thirty-first president (1929–1933), came into office as one of the most qualified men ever to be elected to the presidency. An orphan who grew up unhappy and alone, he was part of the very first class to graduate from Stanford College (now Stanford University). He was a geologist who became one of the great mining engineers of his day. He made fantastic discoveries all over the world, including in China and South America. He had a brilliant organizational mind and led the famine relief effort in Europe after World War I, literally feeding millions of Europeans. He did the same after World War II at the request of President Harry S. Truman, who became Hoover's friend until his death in 1964. He served as Secretary of Commerce for his two immediate predecessors, Warren G. Harding and Calvin Coolidge. When Coolidge decided not to run for reelection in 1928, Hoover was considered a shoo-in and was easily elected.

However, Hoover is considered one of the worst presidents in US history. He wound up inheriting what became the Great Depression from Coolidge, who saw it coming. This is why Coolidge declined to run in 1928. Hoover put in sixteen-hour days at his desk, used his presidential authority to help the economy, brought together some of the finest financial minds in the country to help improve the situation, and proposed all sorts of legislation. He did all he could—and failed miserably.

He had two major problems. He was a micromanager of the highest order. Worse, he was an awful communicator. I've heard some of his speeches myself, and I can tell you that he had the ability to put an insomniac to sleep for a week. He was naturally aloof and uncomfortable around people. Most of the time, he simply sat in his office and refused to see anyone for weeks. When he did speak to the public, he seemed cold and unfeeling. His failure to communicate his actions to the American people and make them realize the extent of his work to reverse the damage of the financial collapse cost him re-election. He was steamrolled by a political meteorite by the name of Franklin Delano Roosevelt.

FDR is widely considered one of the top five greatest US presidents. Born into privileged circumstances, he was an only child who had a natural charm that, combined with his family connections (he was the fifth cousin of President Theodore Roosevelt), set him on a course for an easy life . . . until tragedy struck.

He contracted polio, lost the use of his legs, and was forced into a wheelchair for the remainder of his life. This diagnosis crushed him initially, but he somehow found the strength to reenter the political arena. He ran unsuccessfully as the vice-presidential candidate with James Cox against Warren G. Harding in the 1920 presidential election. He did run successfully for governor of New York and served during Hoover's term of 1929–1933. He had a rather undistinguished term as governor, but his name and position gave him a high launching pad against a very unpopular incumbent. His charm and criticism of Hoover made him an appealing alternative, and he was elected president in a landslide.

Roosevelt inherited Hoover's horrible economy. He instituted a ton of new federal programs, some of which still exist today, such as the Tennessee Valley Authority. Despite all of his work, the Depression lingered until the beginning of the US involvement in World War II at the end of 1941.

So, what was the difference? Why is FDR a revered figure in American history while Hoover is largely forgotten and scorned? Much of the difference has to do with FDR's greatest strength—his ability to communicate. He had a warmth and ebullience about him that allowed him to communicate with the American people in a way that eased their fears. One of his greatest lines, of course, was, "The only thing we have to fear is fear itself."

His regular "Fireside Chats" used the then-new medium known as radio, which brought his voice into people's homes and reassured them that everything was on its way to recovery. It might not have necessarily been true, but it didn't matter. Roosevelt made people feel better by his manner and ability to communicate with the nation. He is our longest-serving President (1933–1945).

Whether you are President of the United States or the leader of your own company or organization, effective communication is essential.

I recently was in contact with a leader who follows me in the JTD Coaching Facebook group. He wrote me a rather nasty note explaining that he thought my views on effective communication were "a bunch of garbage" (for the record, I've cleaned up his language a little). When I asked him how he communicated with his people, he explained quite simply, "I give the orders, loudly. They either do what they're told the way I tell them to do it, or they're gone. Period."

I wished him well and bookmarked his comment. About six weeks later, I checked his profile, and discovered that it now read: "Former business owner. Now unemployed." I think I know part of what caused his demise. A consequence of his style of leadership is that no one has the chance to make an input or comment on what is going on within the company. As time goes on, there is no buy-in and thus, no loyalty. In fact, that type of communication will eventually cause employees to look for an exit strategy.

Effective communication isn't a natural skill for everyone. Like any other skill, it can be improved. A crystal-clear leader goes beyond standard improvement to reach mastery.

The Crystal-Clear Leader's Guide to Effective Communication

A crystal-clear leader:

- Is visible around employees, giving encouragement and offering help as needed
- Regularly engages with employees, customers, and partners
- Regularly communicates the company mission and employee expectations with perfect clarity
- Sets clear goals and objectives for the company and keeps employees appraised of progress as well as issues that arise over time
- Communicates in an honest, straightforward, and friendly manner that shows care and concern for the people he or she leads
- Listens to feedback

Questions and Exercises:

1. Are you fully aware of what everyone in your company or organization wants and needs from you as a leader?

2. If the answer is "no" or "I don't know," what can you do to improve on that?

3. Same questions as numbers one and two above, only this time, apply them to customers and clients.

4. Are your company's goals and objectives perfectly clear to the people you lead?

5. Name three areas of improvement you can and will make in the area of effective communication.

CHAPTER SEVEN
The Ability to Listen

The last foundational skill for the crystal-clear leader is the ability to listen. It may be last, but it certainly isn't least. In fact, I would go so far as to say a leader who is a poor listener will fail as a leader.

Your ability to listen might be the most important skill you possess. A leader who is a good listener just might *learn* something. The key is to do more than just *hear*—you must understand the meaning behind the words. And when a leader learns something, as it was in my case, the difference can be great success.

My company, JTD Coaching and Consulting, is very different from the company I thought I was founding. In fact, if you had told me this company would be what it is now even a few months ago, I'd have said one word: *impossible.* My original concept was to build a speaking business based on the teaching of John Maxwell. The concept made sense, and John Maxwell is an exceptional author and speaker. He is known worldwide for his dozens of excellent books on leadership. The simple idea was to become a John Maxwell speaker within his organization.

It didn't turn out that way, even though I continue to maintain my great respect for John Maxwell and his teaching. What happened? There were four key points during the process that changed everything. In reality, there were four *discussions* at the beginning of and during my personal and professional journey into a brand-new career in my late forties. Had I not listened, and listened carefully, I'd have missed out on three great breaks that changed everything.

The first conversation involved financial planning. Early on, my COO and I were reviewing financial projections based on building a speaking career with one affiliation. The numbers were lucrative, but I wanted to build something more for myself and others. I had no other options at the time, and my COO was worried about the future. I tried to downplay some of the concerns she had. I remained optimistic and didn't admit I shared some of the same concerns.

The second conversation turned out to be life-altering. It was a conversation I had with my friend Brian Tracy at the end of his speaking academy in the fall of 2018, as mentioned in an earlier chapter. As a reminder, it went like this: "Eric, you are good enough to make a living as a speaker. You are as good as ninety-seven percent of the speakers that are in the business. But if you want more than that, if you want to be great at what you do and stand apart from the crowd, you have work to do. You need to put in the effort and develop your speaking skills and knowledge of leadership by that additional three percent. You aren't there yet."

Brian generously made his entire library of trainings and courses available to me. I listened to his advice and went to work. I read his *Maximum Achievement Principles* book and then signed up for his Total Business Mastery course. I increased my knowledge across the board exponentially. I needed to learn a lot more than an extra 3 percent. Brian was kind enough *not* to say that. Brian also graciously has given me permission to teach his Maximum Achievement Principles, which I am incorporating into a new course I'm designing called The CEO Shift. Needless to say, I'm very grateful for his help and support.

Conversation number three was with another friend and mentor—Jack Canfield. Jack is world-renowned for his *Chicken Soup for the Soul* book series. He's also known for his life-changing book *The Success Principles*. I was fortunate enough to take his Success Principles: Train the Trainer course and get certified to teach it myself. When that was finished, Jack informed me that the course contained coaching credits from the International Coach Federation (an organization I had never heard of). He asked me if I had any interest in becoming a professional coach. If so, he said he would direct me to the appropriate place. I informed him I was a professional speaker, and while I was intrigued, I was unsure if it would be a good fit for me. He responded by telling me that I absolutely could become an excellent coach and I should give his suggestion serious thought.

The result: Eric Jackier, Owner and Chief Executive Officer (CEO) of JTD Coaching. I now hold several different coaching credentials that help people achieve greater success than they ever thought possible. It's one of the best decisions I've ever made. I also offer a training that will help other coaches build successful businesses and achieve their own definition of excellence. I love coaching and am proud to say I am now a coach who speaks professionally.

Jack Canfield was nice enough to invite me on his television show *Talking About Success*. You can visit www.jtdcoaching.com to see my most recent interview with Jack.

The fourth and final conversation came during a session I had with my own coach, Ann Babiarz. Ann has become a great friend and colleague. Several months into working with her (through the Tracy-Canfield Coaching program), we were discussing my plans to build the original concept of the speaking business. Ann asked me a question that eventually had a huge impact on me and my business model: "Why are you content with teaching someone else's material and speaking about it when you are fully capable of developing your own original material?" My answer was very clever, as I recall: "How can I possibly do that?"

It's taken a long time, but I have now written four workbooks and the book you are reading now. I have also developed my own original teaching and leadership material. My goal is to help leaders become the best they can possibly be. In other words, a crystal-clear leader! Because I learned to really listen to my coaches and mentors, I've been able to achieve a level of success I only dreamed about when I started out.

Questions and Exercises:

1. Do your employees consider you a good listener? It's important to find out. Ask for confidential feedback.

2. When has a failure to listen led to problems in your personal or business life?

3. Name some important points in your business career in which listening to advice changed the trajectory of your career.

4. Once you complete question one, call a meeting with your employees and then another one with your repeat customers. What are some suggestions they have for you that can help grow and improve your business?

PART TWO

Leadership Responsibilities

CHAPTER EIGHT
Vision

A great way to illustrate *vision* is through a story of a man who fundamentally changed how the world works, as told by someone who witnessed the change despite having never met him.

When I was in high school and then college, computers, while not rare, were certainly not quite common. They were large, clunky machines that mostly ran on a language called NBASIC. My college had eight or ten computers, which meant that maybe six of them worked. If you wanted to use one, you had to schedule time in the AV (audio visual) room and hope and pray a working computer was available. If you couldn't type well, you could always hire someone to do it for you since there were time limits on the use of the computers. That could become expensive, ranging from fifty to 150 dollars. I learned to tolerate typing.

I recently went back to my alma mater, the University of Miami. Everything looked entirely different; thirty years will do that. The only place that looked remotely familiar was where I used to live. I walked over there and told the nice young lady at the desk I was an alum who lived there back in the late 1980s. She welcomed me back and showed me around. Most of it looked familiar, except for one thing—no AV room. When I asked her where it was, she looked at me like I'd come from outer space. She didn't know what an AV room was. I had a feeling I knew why.

My next stop was the bookstore, which was certainly very different than when I was there. It had expanded to three levels from two. When I asked what they carried on the new floor, the answer was computers, tablets, and computer programs.

This happened because one man had a vision: "Everyone should have a personal computer of their own and a program that it runs on." That sixteen-word vision by a gentleman named Bill Gates is what became the Microsoft Corporation.

Without a vision, you can't lead a business or organization of any kind well. It's like trying to hit an invisible moving target.

Please also keep in mind that *vision* is different from *mission*; we'll address mission in the next chapter.

A vision is the result of what you want to accomplish for yourself or organization.

It's that simple—and that complicated. The complications arise when the vision becomes clouded. It can happen simply due to the activity and tasks of daily life—new projects and opportunities, a new business venture that may not match the vision but might make money, and so forth. When that happens, it's up to the leader to refocus everything back on the vision.

Don't mistake clarity of the vision for rigid adherence to the vision. It is entirely acceptable for a vision to change as circumstances and conditions change. I guarantee that every leader will encounter situations that require an unexpected pivot. The vision of four months ago may not be the vision now. The same might be said three months from now. You must be adroit and flexible as conditions change.

My own vision for myself and my company has changed over the last year. The original vision was to build a speaking business based on the teaching of John Maxwell. That vision is now extinct.

My new vision is this: "To build a world-class coaching and leadership development company that helps struggling leaders improve and good leaders become exceptional." For the record, writing this chapter helped me clarify my vision for JTD Coaching. This is the first time this statement has ever been written. That's powerful!

Questions and Exercises:

1. What is your current vision for your business or organization?

2. Do your employees have professional visions for themselves or your company? Ask them.

3. Do you have your vision and mission statements confused? This question will reappear at the end of the next chapter.

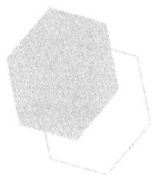

CHAPTER NINE

Mission

Now that we've tackled vision, let's take a look at mission. These two should never be confused, but unfortunately, they often are. I've done it myself! Let's do some comparisons.

> **Vision: "A personal computer with a program that runs it for everyone."**

That was Bill Gates's vision.

Now, let's examine a *mission* statement from another world-famous CEO you may have heard of by the name of Jack Welch:

> **Mission: "We will be number one or number two in all of our businesses. Those businesses that cannot achieve that will be sold off or shut down."**

That statement became the General Electric (GE) mission for twenty years.

Now, let's look at the subtle but major difference between the two. The vision Bill Gates had is what became Microsoft's *purpose*. The mission Jack Welch created for GE defined how the company *operated*.

To further illustrate, I'll use my company as an example:

> **Vision: "To build a world-class coaching and leadership development company that will help struggling leaders improve and good leaders become exceptional."**

Mission: "JTD Coaching will provide premium coaching and leadership development programs—both individually and in small groups—for leaders who are looking to improve their skills and successful leaders who are looking to become exceptional."

Each of the statements above are critical for a crystal-clear leader as they begin to build a successful company or organization. A leader must spend ample time, literally as much time as is needed, to make sure of two things:

1. The vision and mission must be two separate elements that are not confusing or intertwined.
2. Both statements must have complete *clarity*.

We will discuss the importance of clarity in the next chapter. I will gladly confess to the reader that in writing this and the previous chapter, I coached myself and improved my vision and mission statements for JTD. I hope I did the same for you.

Questions and Exercises:

1. Review your company or organizational mission statement. What are your thoughts after reviewing it? Does it need updating or revising?

2. Do you have your vision and mission statements confused? Using the different examples from this chapter, what can you do to provide complete clarity for both?

3. If applicable, write a brand-new mission statement for your company. What makes this new one different from the previous one?

CHAPTER TEN

Clarity

Now it's time for you to develop your own Crystal-Clear Clarity Plan. Your plan should contain the following elements:

Company name:

Owner/CEO:

Responsibilities only the CEO must handle:

Key executives:

List the functions and responsibilities of each key executive as you see them:

Ask each of the executives to list their functions and responsibilities:

List each employee by name:

List their key responsibilities:

Do we need to keep everyone we have?

Do we need to hire additional people?

Ask each employee to list their responsibilities:

What are our primary products and services?

Do each of the products and services achieve the financial goals we set for them?

Are we hitting our sales goals? (need input for this)

Who is our ideal client and customer?

Who are our best customers and clients?

How much repeat business can we expect from them over the next six to twelve months?

Who among our other clients and customers might graduate into the top category?

What can we do to get them to that level? (Get input from top executives and sales team.)

What additional products or services can we introduce over the next six months, twelve months, and eighteen months to increase our revenue streams?

How much will we need to invest to bring these to the market?

Do we have the funds available to accomplish our short-, medium-, and long-term goals?

When you can answer the questions above with clarity, you will have achieved what you need to take your leadership and your business or organization to new heights of success and excellence. You will also reap the additional benefits of beginning to set goals and construct your strategic planning process, which will be discussed in the next chapters.

Questions and Exercises:

1. Answer the questions in the Crystal-Clear Clarity Plan. Collect the answers from your key people and employees.

2. What surprised you about your own answers and the answers from everyone else?

3. As a leader, are you operating with clarity?

4. Is your company or organization operating with clarity?

5. Knowing what you now know, what actions do you as a leader need to take to bring more clarity to your employees?

CHAPTER ELEVEN

Goal Setting

Question: What is the goal of every professional sports team?
Answer: To win the championship.

Most human beings strive to accomplish something each day. The days become weeks, months, years, and so forth. We strive to succeed. We want to get married, have a family, buy a house, build a business, retire comfortably. Each of these are examples of goals.

Every business has goals—they must. Much like the discussion we had about clarity in the previous chapter, it's the job of the leader to set the goals as well as set the course for how those goals will be reached.

Is this a goal? I want to make a million dollars per year.

Well, so do I. So do a few hundred million others. But this is not a goal. It's a wish. Let's look at another statement.

Is this a goal? I want to make a million dollars per year within the next five years.

Yes, that is a goal. However, there is still something missing in the above statement—a way to accomplish the goal.

A top-flight leader understands that an achievement process to reaching these goals—otherwise known as a "goal-setting process"—must always be included in the planning and execution of goals.

Let's break this down in its simplest terms, something the leader must always do well to avoid confusion.

There are three types of goals:

- Short-term (three months)

- Medium-term (six to twelve months)
- Long-term (one to two years)

Additionally, there are three goal definitions within the goals above. Let's define them very clearly so you can begin setting up your refined goal-setting system.

- **Achievable goals** are goals that can and should be achieved within a time frame or deadline, usually thirty to ninety days. Barring a crisis within the company or something unforeseen that may change the goal itself, completion is to be successfully attained.
- **Reach goals** are those that can be attained, but it might take longer than the desired time frame, normally six to twelve months. Accomplishing the goal sooner rather than later would be a win for the leader, team, and company. It is usually a goal you would *like* to achieve in the short-term that may or may not be possible depending on the existing conditions and realities of the company.
- **Stretch goals** are over one year away. A stretch goal is something to strive for as time goes on. Achieving a stretch goal is a game-changing situation for all involved.

Questions and Exercises:

1. What are some key short-, medium-, and long-term goals for your company or organization?

2. Which categories do these goals fall under—achievable, reach, or stretch?

3. Are your key people and employees familiar with how these goals were set and why?

4. Do they buy into these goals?

5. Having examined the goal-setting process, do any of your goals need to be reexamined?

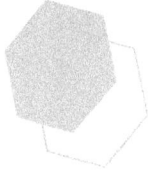

CHAPTER TWELVE
Strategic Planning

You may have already noticed we're following an important pattern. The previous four chapters on vision, mission, clarity, and goal-setting have now brought us to the next step in the sequence. This step is an especially important one. Now that you know where you want to go, how exactly will you plan to get there? A good strategic plan is your roadmap for reaching your goals.

In his renowned High Performance Leadership program, Brian Tracy asks a series of important questions that need to be answered when building a strategic plan. Under each of his questions, I'll add a few suggestions. Between the two of us, you will have the tools you need to build a crystal-clear strategic plan.

How did I get here today?

When answering this question, be excruciatingly honest about the condition of your company. Take ownership, even if it's uncomfortable. Once that's done, picture this day as a launching point. And it is! You are on your way to an excellent strategic plan!

Where do I want to go?

You should have a pretty good idea of that based on the work we've done in the last four chapters. It never hurts to go back over everything in order to cross-check your vision, mission, and the clarity of your goals and objectives. Once done, you are ready to answer this question.

How do I get there?

That's what we are working on now in this chapter.

What are the industry trends?

Make sure you're very clear on this answer. This is a mistake I made with my last business. I didn't see—or maybe I *refused* to see—the industry trends. As a result, I was unsuccessful and quickly became obsolete. Part of what makes a crystal-clear leader is more than merely knowing the industry trends; it's having the foresight to identify future industry trends and putting your company at the forefront. Let's add two more questions that will make the difference.

- What will the industry trends be in the next one to three years?
- How can my company set those trends?

What are the constraints?

Identify them, write them down, then figure out how to remove them. For example, if the constraint is a financial one, can you eliminate a recurring expense that might remove the constraint? This happened to me recently. An opportunity was presented to me to onboard an information services company that would help me identify qualified leads for my group coaching business. The expense was prohibitive. But when I was shown the true impact of what this company could do, I immediately went through all the standing monthly expenses I have and found three I could get rid of. Now not only can I now afford to hire the information services company, but I will also actually save nearly two thousand dollars per month in overall expenses. Constraint removed.

What additional skills will you need?

My answer to this question is to identify them and acquire them. As a leader, you must never allow your skills, talents, and knowledge to become obsolete or secondary. The same is true for your company. If they do, you've had it.

What are the obstacles?

Obstacles are usually more difficult than constraints. Obstacles are similar to roadblocks. In business cases, it can be a competitor that is larger or more well-funded, a valued employee who may ask for a large raise in order to avoid leaving for a competitor, or a flaw in your sales process. Whatever the obstacle, I'm a believer that if you can't go around it, over it, or under it, find a way to go through it, as long as it's legal and ethical.

What is your competitive advantage?

Another way to ask this is "Why should a customer buy from you as opposed to the competition?" You must be able to answer this question with complete clarity.

What is your area of excellence?

What can you do better than anyone else in your field of expertise? You need to answer this question with complete clarity too.

What are your core competencies?

As a leader, what are you good at? Again, write it down. I would also list your weaknesses or areas for improvement. You might also ask your key employees to answer this question.

What must the leader become to build a successful company?

This is another nonnegotiable question. You must invest in improving your core competencies. It's an investment in yourself and the success of your business. Identify what you must do and include it in your budget.

Who are your competitors?

It would serve you well to familiarize yourself as best you can with your competitors' core competencies, areas of excellence, competitive advantages, obstacles, and constraints. While you certainly won't be able to find out everything you might want to know, as the old saying goes, "The better you know your competition, the more successful you will be." It's true.

Are you the best?

I might ask this question a little differently: What do I have to do to become the best or maintain my ability to be the best?

Do you ask the right questions?

Only you as the leader knows this answer, so I can't advise you on it. You may look for feedback from your clients and employees. That's a good question to ask!

Questions and Exercises:

1. Take some time to answer Brian's questions along with the ones I added.

2. Using those answers, begin to construct your strategic plan.

3. Once done, evaluate the following:
   a) Is the plan practical?
   b) Do I have the resources to execute the plan?
   c) What are the timetables, deadlines, and tools needed to make the plan work?

An important note: Make sure the timetables and deadlines are included in the strategic plan. Without them, it's not a strategic plan—it's a wish list. That defeats the whole purpose of the exercise. Without a strategic plan, you cannot achieve the results you desire.

CHAPTER THIRTEEN

Management Responsibilities

Leadership and management are similar to the relationship between siblings. They have similarities but are not quite the same. However, it's worth discussing the importance of excellent management in this book, too, because it's the role of the crystal-clear leader to provide top-flight management.

If you're looking for something outstanding to read in the field of management, read anything written by Peter Drucker; I especially recommend *The Practice of Management*. I would also recommend the book *Winning* by Jack Welch, which provides a very practical guide to business management.

It's very important for leaders to be mindful of two critical factors when it comes to leadership and management:

1. **The leader sets the management tone, tasks, and objectives.**
2. **The leader delegates the tasks; they do not perform them.**

The Tasks of Management as Directed by the Crystal-Clear Leader

- **Planning** – Quite literally, the leader must map and chart the organization's course.
- **Goal-Setting** – As we discussed in an earlier chapter, the leader should set the goals of the organization with appropriate deadlines, timelines, and measurements that help gauge success.

- **Organization** – The leader must direct how the business will run. This includes deciding who is responsible for certain tasks, how products and services will be delivered, and how that delivery will happen.
- **Staffing** – The leader is responsible for finding, interviewing, hiring (or in many cases, approving new hires), and putting new employees in a position to succeed.
- **Delegation** – The leader must lead and assign the tasks that need to be performed by others.
- **Supervision** – The leader is ultimately responsible for making sure everything gets done on time and to the highest standard possible.
- **Standards of Performance** – The leader is ultimately responsible for the reputation of the company or organization they lead and the people they employ.
- **Effective Communication** – The leader must know how to communicate effectively. They should also know how the people they work with like their information disseminated.
- **Solution-Oriented** – People look to the leader to be the problem solver and find solutions.
- **Continuous Improvement** – The crystal-clear leader always demands improvement. This includes improvement from the leader, the people who work with and for them, and within and throughout the company or organization they lead. Leaders keep things moving forward. All the time.

Questions and Exercises:

1. Look at the list of management tasks on the previous page. What are your management strengths?

2. What are your management weaknesses?

3. Define three areas where your organization can improve its management processes.

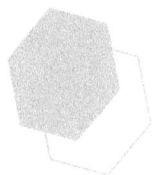

CHAPTER FOURTEEN
Team-Building

If you're a sports fan like me, you know the importance of having a good team around you. The greatest team I've ever seen is the New York Yankees from 1996–2001. They won four out of six World Series in that span of time, and they came very close to winning all six. No team has ever made me prouder!

It's every bit as important to build a good team around *yourself* too. This skill, if done right, can make you and your company the New York Yankees of your industry.

As we will discuss shortly, you won't be able to delegate effectively if you don't have good people on your team, so becoming a crystal-clear team-builder is an essential skill.

I've been reading a book called *Chumps to Champs*, which details the rebuilding and resurgence of the New York Yankees in the 1990s. One of the more interesting chapters in the book explains the conversion of Jorge Posada from an infielder to a championship catcher who became one of the iconic Yankees of his generation.

Posada had a lot to learn about the nuances of the catching position. He did have several important attributes, though: an excellent arm, a live bat, and natural leadership tendencies. He became a very vocal leadership presence in the clubhouse, often saying things on behalf of Derek Jeter, the legendary team captain. He asked a lot of questions and worked hard on improving his footwork, receiving skills, and knowledge of pitchers.

When asked years later why they would convert a natural infielder like Posada into a catcher, Bill Livesey—then the Yankees' director of international scouting—said the following, "Skills can be taught. Top-flight team players are hard to find."

The architect of those great Yankee teams was Gene "Stick" Michael. He took over the Yankees at their lowest point in the team's glorious history. He knew very well that the entire organization needed to be completely rebuilt.

When it comes to building excellent teams, I have five fundamentals I use. I thank Brian Tracy, Jack Canfield, and the late great Coach Wooden—whom, sadly, I never had the opportunity to meet—for teaching me the ropes. Many of my ideas were developed from their teachings.

Using the five fundamentals of team building, let's examine how Michael applied them to building the Yankees of the late 1990s to the early 2000s.

- **The selection of team members is vital:** This was a particular strength of both Michael and his manager, Buck Showalter. Their selection was based not only on whom they chose to be on the team, but also whom they removed. They were looking for a certain kind of team member—players who were dedicated to working hard and winning every day. If someone was just putting in time in and collecting a paycheck, they weren't going to last long.
- **Identify the team leader:** Derek Jeter became that leader for the Yankees. He set the tone for the entire team over a twenty-year period. He also seemed to always come through when it counted.
- **The leader must set the expectations for the team:** It was "World Series or bust" every year. That demand was made by the team's legendary owner, the late George Steinbrenner. Nothing short of achieving the goal was acceptable. On the field, Jeter set a similar tone.
- **The team must expect to be the best:** The team members often said they expected to win every day. This is particularly true of the team in 1998. They went 125–50 that year, an incredible record! Many consider that team to be the greatest of all time.
- **The team members should feel appreciated and rewarded:** Whether it's financial, public recognition, or maybe a promotion, over twenty years later, every single member of that team is fondly remembered and continues to reap the benefits of having been part of the greatest team of all time.

The example of the great Yankees teams of the 1990s and 2000s provide a larger-than-life example when it comes to team-building. Most of us can never imagine building teams to those heights. When you're the leader of any organization, it's important to build teams of very high quality.

But to build teams to the crystal-clear standard, the five fundamentals of team building are not enough. As a leader, you need to do more.

A crystal-clear leader knows how to put the team members in their correct positions for the team and the company to succeed. There are so many stories of people who have failed in one role only to succeed in another. Often this has happened within the same company. It's always wise when hiring to do a skills analysis or aptitude test. I use Coach Wooden's Pyramid of Success skills evaluation quiz; it's the best I've ever seen of its kind. I use the StrengthsFinder test on occasion as well. It also never hurts to ask the employee what role they prefer.

A crystal-clear leader will invest the necessary resources to develop the team and its members. The best teams in the world haven't got a chance if they don't have the tools to succeed. This includes finances, technology, products, and so forth. A prime example of this is the Cincinnati Bengals, an NFL team.

The NFL offers revenue sharing and the richest national television contracts of any of the four major sports. The league swims in money.

The Bengals are perennially unsuccessful. They haven't won a playoff game in nearly thirty years! Why are they consistently so awful? A major part of the problem is that their facilities are considered the worst in the league by a mile. They still use an outdoor practice field that has been in use since the 1960s, and it gets awfully cold in Ohio in the winter. Their stadium has been upgraded, but nowhere near to the level of the AT&T Stadium, where the Dallas Cowboys play, or the new stadiums that have been built in Las Vegas for the Raiders or Los Angeles for the Rams and Chargers. The facilities in Cincinnati where the Bengals play are considered third-rate and decades behind the other facilities in the league. Players simply don't want to play there if they have a choice.

A similar thing can happen in an organization that doesn't keep up. The best and most competent people will go elsewhere. A crystal-clear leader doesn't make this mistake.

Questions and Exercises:

1. Are you familiar with your employees' strengths and weaknesses? Where do they fit if they are part of a team?

2. Using the five fundamentals of team-building, analyze whether your people are operating in the right places. What conclusions have you drawn?

3. In what ways are you, as a leader, supporting your best teams and team members?

4. What is your plan to continue to invest to ensure retention of your best team members? Be specific.

5. Analyze the quality of your team. Are they people of high character? Are they dedicated to the point where they will put in extra time and effort to make your company more successful? How do they relate and react to one another?

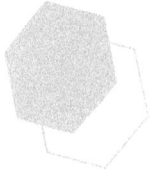

CHAPTER FIFTEEN

Staffing

Perhaps the single most important decision a leader makes is who they bring into their organization. Remember, the most important and expensive assets you have are your *people*.

The solo entrepreneur might say, "I work alone. Why do I need to worry about staffing?"

The answer is this—if you work alone, completely alone, you will not succeed. I'm living proof of that. For all the leaders must know and do well to achieve crystal-clear success, there isn't a leader in the world who knows everything they need to know or does everything well. The crystal-clear leader knows this and, with that understanding, appropriately staffs their company.

As I said, I'm living proof a leader cannot work alone if they expect to succeed. The idea that you must do everything yourself and do it well isn't only absurd—it's fatal to success. There are at least three people every leader needs to work with to be successful:

- **Personal assistant**—This is preferably someone who has two primary assets:
  1. A skill set that complements and enhances the skills of the leader.
  2. The ability to take on tasks or projects they can handle better than the leader. At the very least, those tasks and projects should allow the leader to focus on the work only they should be doing.
- **Attorney**—As unpleasant as it is to think about, in today's world everyone needs to have a lawyer on speed dial. You never know when a legal issue will arise and, worse, who and where it

will come from. The leader must be prepared for anything. Like it or not, an attorney is a must.

- **Accountant**—At the very least, it never hurts to have someone on the team besides the leader to check and recheck the numbers, make sure the bills are paid, and deal with everyone's friend: the tax man. Sooner or later, an accountant will be needed. Protect yourself before you need to.

Now, let's talk about bringing in and—when necessary—removing people from the organization. Picking the right people to bring into your organization is as critical as anything else you will do as a leader. If you've noticed a pattern throughout this book, I like processes and organization. The crystal-clear leader definitely needs to have processes in place for this area of the business.

The Power of Three

Here are my rules for hiring someone at JTD Coaching; I call it the power of three. My system requires these three processes to occur before anyone is hired.

- Three candidates
- Three interviews
- Three approvals

Three Candidates

The last thing in the world any leader should do is rush into a hire. If you bring someone in too quickly, you might have to replace them just as quickly. That costs time, money, and productivity. Ideally, you are looking for someone who is:

- Honest and reliable
- Experienced in the job they are interviewing for (although you can be flexible if they show high intelligence and growth potential)

- Friendly and professional with an ability to work well with others and be part of a team
- Looking for a long-term position

Three Interviews

Hiring is about adding to your team. My definition of a good-to-excellent hire is someone who brings competence and skills that can help further the company mission. A learning and growth mindset is something to be valued. When you spot that type of mindset, do what you can to help them do just that: learn and grow. Also, remember to acknowledge, appreciate, and reward outstanding performance. An enthusiastic employee who feels appreciated will usually go the extra mile to help the company succeed. When you have that, you and your company win!

A potential candidate will first interview with the people who plan and run my seminars and appearances. They are very familiar with every aspect of JTD. They are empowered to recommend and also veto any candidate without having to receive approval from me or my COO.

The second interview belongs to the COO. She is not only well-versed in the company, but also has intimate knowledge about working with me and my expectations. She, too, has full autonomy to veto or continue. If she recommends the candidate, the final interview is with me.

Three Approvals

At this point, I will have the recommendations I need as well as the candidate's aptitude skills test and evaluations. I will also take my team's thoughts on the four points listed above very seriously. I will only meet someone if everyone else approves. What I'm looking for is confirmation of the recommendations from everyone along with forming my own idea of where the person will fit into JTD. For the record, if I'm uncomfortable, I'll veto, and we will start over again. If we're lucky and everyone grades well, we'll either bring the person back for a group interview or we'll meet by ourselves and make a collective and collaborative decision.

This may sound like a lot of involvement and investment of time in the hiring process, and it is. It is also a critical function of leadership to get it right the first time. I've learned that it takes a lot more time, and expense, if I get it wrong.

When the hire is made, the new employee receives a welcome letter signed by my COO and by me. It should include all pertinent details of the hire, including confirmation of salary, job description and responsibilities, company policies, and so forth. As a final step, the new hire signs off on it. All this does is add that final step of clarity, something you absolutely want when onboarding a new employee.

The Flip side of the Process: Removal

Removal is harder, of course, and can be tricky if things aren't handled correctly. You should have a warning system in place for employees before the termination process is activated. First, I recommend a meeting with the employee, the immediate report, and the supervisor. If the process is elevated to the next step, a warning letter should be written and signed by the same three participants. If all else fails, the termination process should be activated.

There are two types of termination. The standard type involves issues such as poor job performance, chronic absence, budget cuts, and so forth. In these cases, there should always be previous documentation that addresses these points, as discussed above. I strongly recommend contacting your attorney before firing anyone so all legal precautions can be taken on behalf of the company or organization. There should also be a signed document at the end of the final discussion with the terms, causes, and so forth spelled out. Remember to be as kind and considerate as possible when terminating someone; it is very traumatic for everyone involved.

The second type of termination is immediate. This occurs, of course, when someone must be removed instantly. Again, call your lawyer as soon as possible. Protect yourself and your company. I will immediately remove an employee for the following reasons:

- Theft
- Lying or disinformation

- Illegal activity of any kind
- Violence or the threat of it from an employee to anyone involved with the company
- Inappropriate behavior (unwanted sexual advances, inappropriate humor, etc.)

In cases like these, the employee must be removed immediately and escorted from the premises, never to be allowed back in.

There is always the question of which day of the week is best to remove someone. My choice would be Tuesday. It gives you a day to prepare and review everything down to the last period. It also shows compassion to the person being removed, as it gives them the majority of the remaining week to recover and begin their job search rather than be angry and stew about the situation over the weekend. The other advantage of a Tuesday is it also allows the remaining employees to deal with the change while also adjusting to whatever new role they may have in the company.

Questions and Exercises:

1. What is your company's hiring process?

2. What is your company's removal process?

3. What are the top five qualities you look for when hiring a candidate?

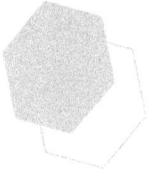

CHAPTER SIXTEEN

Delegation

This is a good time for a little review, similar to Coach Wooden's Pyramid of Success. Every step should build on the previous one, and the fundamentals must be mastered before we keep going.

A crystal-clear leader has a clear vision, has created a mission as to how the company will operate, understands where both the leader and the company needs to go with unwavering clarity, and has a strategic plan that will act as the roadmap.

At this point, however, there is a trap right in front of you. It's a major mistake leaders make all the time—I call it the micromanagement trap.

The micromanagement trap is a leadership and success killer, and I mean that literally. There isn't a leader in the world who is capable of doing every single business task well or successfully. Additionally, looking over your employees' shoulders as they work, not allowing them to take ownership of their work and responsibilities, and constantly correcting them both privately and in front of others can slow or halt productivity and increase employee turnover. All that does is sidetrack production and accomplishment. It can also lead to high company turnover, which naturally can grind a strategic plan to a halt.

A fundamental skill for any crystal-clear leader is the ability to delegate. Delegate absolutely everything except what only you can and must do.

It sounds simple, right? It can be, especially if your staff has been with you a long time and works well together. However, be careful—there's another trap that can spring itself on the leader: over-delegation.

Over-delegation occurs when the leader simply washes his hands of a task, doesn't give guidance or set deadlines for completion, or doesn't track appropriate progress. When this occurs, it's every bit as bad as the micro-management trap.

The crystal-clear leader creates a delegation system. Here is how mine works.

The Crystal-Clear Leader's Twelve-Step Delegation System

1. Identify the task to be delegated.
2. Decide on the timetable for task completion.
3. When possible, break down the overall task or project into smaller subprojects.
4. Write down the names of the key people who might potentially handle the task.
5. Decide who can complete the task successfully. If the task will take more than one person, divide the work accordingly. If the person is new, perhaps give them less to do until both you and they are comfortable.
6. Meet with your team and assign the task.
7. Put the task in writing and insist that your staff do the same. This simply eliminates misunderstandings. You'd be amazed what can get lost in translation. When you delegate an important task, misunderstandings cannot happen.
8. Communicate your deadlines and expectations with absolute clarity. Make sure those are written down too.
9. Empower your employees to solve problems as they arise.
10. Set up regular points of contact or regular meetings to track progress, answer questions, and provide oversight. Until then, leave them alone.
11. Make absolutely sure you have given your people the resources they need to get the job done.
12. If you don't have the appropriate people to handle the task, then treat it as work you as the leader must do and DO NOT delegate the task. Giving a task to someone who can't get the job done effectively is disastrous for everyone involved.

This fundamental process is crucial for the success of the leader and the organization. If delegating is a process that makes you uncomfortable, my advice would be to start by assigning smaller tasks and build from there.

Questions and Exercises:

1. List two to three tasks you might delegate to your key people or employees.

2. Identify those key people.

3. Review the twelve-step delegation process. Where are some of the areas you might improve within this process?

CHAPTER SEVENTEEN

Time Management

What do all of us have in common with Bill Gates, Jeff Bezos, and Warren Buffett as leaders? (One hint—it's not our bank accounts.)

The answer to this question is we all have the same twenty-four hours, seven days per week, 365 days per year that they do. It all comes down to how we use and manage our time.

The way we deal with time defines our overall effectiveness as leaders. We must use our time wisely in order to be successful. The crystal-clear leader is *organized, focused,* and *task-oriented* when managing their time.

There's nothing fancy about time management. It's one of the most straightforward skills the crystal-clear leader must master. All it really takes to manage time effectively is remembering the three words italicized above. For coaching purposes, I'll repeat them again so we can explore the importance of each.

- Organized
- Focused
- Task-Oriented

Organized

This is the foundation of successful time management. If your time isn't organized, especially as a leader, trouble will follow.

I insist on keeping my own schedule. I know of other leaders whose staff members keep their calendars in order. However your schedule is kept, your calendar should include the following:

- Standing weekly tasks, appointments, and calls
- Daily tasks
- Reading and review time
- Think time

The others are obvious, but let's talk about think time. I make sure I carve out a minimum of three hours per week to simply think. It's the single best and most important task you have as a leader. As you put this practice into place, you'll find you will quickly improve on your strategic planning, decision-making, and clarity—three fundamental skills we've discussed at length in this book.

I will issue you a challenge. Try my think-time process for a month—three hours per week. If you find it hasn't helped you dramatically with your overall productivity, I'll give you a free thirty-minute coaching session. Before you start your process, send me a copy of your weekly schedule so I can track your progress.

Focused

This is centered around something incredibly simple that all leaders struggle with—getting our work done.

We've all heard the old saying, "There aren't enough hours in the day." This statement is true for only one reason: we as leaders allow distractions to steal control of our time.

According to a study Brian Tracy shared with me and my fellow speaking academy students, in an eight-hour workday, only three hours of actual work gets done. That's bad enough when it comes to staff and employees, but it's an unmitigated disaster for a leader. The distractions are all the same. Phone calls that seem urgent but aren't. Social media, which I think was invented to cut down on production, not to mention drive the world crazy. People dropping by the office who "need two minutes" and stay for twenty. All this lost production time adds up!

What you must do is set boundaries. It's up to you to keep control of your time. If you are unable to do that by yourself, designate someone on your staff (or someone close to you) to act as gatekeeper to avoid and eliminate distractions.

When I have a task that must absolutely be completed, I make sure I eliminate all distractions:

- I don't take any calls.
- I shut down my phone and put my iPad on "Do Not Disturb" to avoid the alerts, noise, and so forth. Remember, every distraction can cost you twenty minutes of productivity.
- I close my door so no one disturbs me.

Task-Oriented

This is the natural continuation point from being focused. Once you reach the point of total focus, you must train that focus on the completion of the tasks you as the leader are responsible for. I was able to sharpen this skill when I started writing workbooks.

The writing process requires a great amount of concentration. On top of that, there's almost always a heavy research component that goes along with it. Before I start researching and writing, I go through this thorough process:

- I define the entire task or project from start to finish.
- I break the task down into weekly and daily pieces.
- I define how many hours I estimate it will take to complete the work. Then I set the necessary time aside.
- My weekly and daily schedule reflects the tasks to be completed. I make every reasonable effort to complete my tasks.

This process works with any sort of task or project. As you read this chapter and my process, it might strike you as simplistic and obvious. It isn't. Putting excellent time management into action, then weaving it into your regular leadership routine takes a lot of hard work and practice. But I guarantee that if you master your time, you will see your personal and professional results skyrocket to new heights of productivity. That's a win for everyone, including your company!

Questions and Exercises:

1. Examine any standard week. Try and keep track of all the distractions and instances when you were pulled away from something important. How much production time did you lose this week?

2. Now, examine the following week. Using the various processes discussed in this chapter, how much production time was recaptured? What were you able to accomplish with the time you took back?

3. Name a task you must complete within a certain time frame. How will you break it down in order to complete it effectively within that time frame?

CHAPTER EIGHTEEN
Crisis Management

Another important component of becoming a crystal-clear leader is knowing how to navigate your business through a crisis. The Coronavirus Pandemic (COVID-19) taught us many important lessons that will make us better business owners in the future. Although I hope we never encounter another pandemic like this in our lifetime, I won't let the tools I've gained through this experience be put to waste—and you'll find they're applicable to most crises you will encounter.

Here are a couple of key points to keep in mind when facing a crisis as the leader of your business or organization.

First, you must make the decision to pull your company, and everyone who depends on it, through the crisis successfully. A healthy mindset must be created before anything else happens. If you make the decision that your company will survive the immediate crisis and become successful once it's over, you will have taken a key step toward making good things happen.

An important point to keep in mind as we move forward is that no one should go through a crisis alone. Every leader should have a group or team of trusted advisors who bring various areas of expertise and experience to the table during a crisis. There is no leader in the world who excels in every single area of leadership.

Now, the real work begins! When handling a crisis, you must plan the recovery and success process. This planning should cover ninety days, the equivalent of a business quarter. However, this plan must be based on fluid assumptions due to the constantly changing situation. The plan should be a living document to be reviewed daily. Each day, the following questions should be asked:

- How long can I stay afloat given the current situation?
- What can I offer the public right now?
- How much cash is available to me?
- Who among my employees is critical to my company's success right now?
- What critical services do I need to provide once the immediate crisis is over?
- Where can I cut costs?

Below are some questions that are less immediate but require clear answers as your ninety-day plan takes shape:

- Is my company eligible for government assistance?
- How should I handle my creditors?
- What should I tell my clients and customers?
- How much money will I realistically make over the next ninety days?
- What are my best- and worst-case scenarios over this period?

As you write your plan, be conservative in your estimates. As an example, while I did think I would have some income and new opportunities during COVID-19, I planned based on having *zero*. Zero-based planning is the safest way to plan during a crisis—especially when everything can be so unpredictable.

As you write your plan, please understand that this kind of business planning is very different from a normal quarterly plan—it's designed for crisis management. Using my model for COVID-19, here's my prescription for a successful crisis management plan:

1. **Work backward.** This may seem counterintuitive, especially since normal business planning requires a leader to look forward. In a crisis situation, you need to visualize the outcome you want to achieve before you do anything else.
2. **Divide by three.** Take the overall outcome you want as the end result and break it down into monthly goals. Think about what

can be accomplished based on the current circumstances within the next thirty days.

3. **Script your month.** Use a monthly calendar for this. Prepare your month using the ideal scenario for crisis recovery. When it's completed, go over it with your crisis management team. Once that's finished, hang it up in a place where you can see it every day. Refer to it frequently.

4. **Weekly breakdown.** At the end of this chapter, you'll find examples of daily and weekly worksheets for you to fill out during a crisis. These questions will make up your ninety-day plan and keep you focused on your goals.

5. **Ground level.** As I'm sure you've figured out, what I'm trying to show you is how to manage the crisis on a granular level. Working backward allows the leader to focus on the business at its roots. Think of your business as a tree. If the roots are strong and healthy, the business—much like a tree—will prosper. You as the leader must ensure that this happens.

Here are some other important tips for building your crisis management plan:

- Be flexible at all times, as the conditions during a crisis can change at any point.
- Keep it simple.
- Focus on what the business does well; figure out how it can deliver results immediately.
- Remove those products and services that have little or no value.
- Make sure you have enough money in the bank to cover ninety days.
- Use zero-based budgeting (based on the idea there will be no revenue for ninety days).
- Build the plan with your best customers in mind.
- Identify your key revenue streams. How quickly can you get them up and running?
- Identify your *key* people and put them to work in executing the plan.
- Make sure you have all the key information; make adjustments as necessary.

- Do a daily review, then do a weekly review.
- Be prepared for anything.

Crisis management is a lot for any leader to handle; the most important thing is to keep calm and lead with strength, courage, and confidence. During COVID-19, every leader in the world was forced to quickly adjust to running a business during a pandemic, but through this process, many of us learned useful lessons for how to guide our businesses and organizations through a crisis. With luck, none of us will ever experience a crisis of this magnitude again, but if we do—we'll be ready.

Questions and Exercises:

The next two exercises detail the daily and weekly worksheets that guided me through the pandemic. If you find yourself facing a disaster, use them well!

Visit *www.jtdcoaching.com* for a printable version of these worksheets

Crisis Management Daily Worksheet: Ninety-Day Plan

Daily tasks:

    1.

    2.

    3.

    4.

    5.

Daily communications:

    1.

    2.

    3.

    4.

    5.

What went well today?

What went wrong?

How am I feeling today as the leader of my business?

What can I do tomorrow better than I did today to keep things moving forward?

Managing the Crisis – Weekly Plan Review

Top five tasks this week

1.
2.
3.
4.
5.

Who can I network with this week in order to create new opportunities in the future?

1.
2.
3.
4.
5.

Who must I communicate with this week? (Staff, creditors, vendors, etc.)

1.

2.

3.

4.

5.

What am I offering (products or services) this week that can help people get through the crisis? (Think about future clients)

1.

2.

3.

What were the company expenses this week?

1.

2.

3.

What was the income?

What are some new projects I can introduce that can bring in revenue?

1.

2.

3.

What have I done this week to steer the company through the crisis?

1.

2.

3.

What must I do next week to make progress?

1.

2.

3.

Additional notes and new ideas

CHAPTER NINETEEN

Flexibility

The winningest coach in the history of the National Football League (NFL) is Don Shula. He coached the Baltimore Colts and the Miami Dolphins. His 347 wins, plus two Super Bowl Championships in 1972 and 1973, include the only undefeated season in NFL history (1972). Shula's passing at the age of ninety brought his incredible accomplishments back to the forefront of the NFL community.

One of the amazing things he did during the 1970s and 1980s was completely change the playing style of his Miami teams. Coach Shula believed in running the football first and foremost, along with an attack-style defense that played with minimal mistakes on both sides of the ball. In the player draft of 1983, right after the Dolphins lost Super Bowl XVII to the Washington Redskins, a strong-armed quarterback by the name of Dan Marino dropped into the Dolphins' lap on the twenty-seventh pick.

Marino had a rifle arm and the quickest release in the history of the league. Before he was finished with his Hall of Fame career, he broke just about every single passing record that existed until three guys named Brady, Manning, and Brees recently broke many of them—twenty-five years later.

Shula quickly realized what he had in Marino and immediately changed his entire offense from run-first into a dynamic passing attack that became the most exciting offense of the mid to late 1980s. Despite Coach Shula being very definitive and committed to his beliefs about running the football, he showed an amazing capacity to change and be *flexible*.

Flexibility is a vitally important skill for a leader. The United States is recovering from the horrific damage inflicted by the coronavirus. Crystal-clear leaders with strong flexibility skills were able to stabilize, pivot, and rebuild their business, as discussed in the previous chapter. A lack of flexibility really wasn't a choice.

To survive unpredictable and unprecedented times, several practices must be adopted. Let's look at the type of flexibility that might be necessary for a crystal-clear leader.

Staff Flexibility – The leader must adapt in a way that allows staff members to be productive in various environments (at home, in the office, online). While doing so, the staff must understand in no uncertain terms that the deadlines set and quality of work are to be maintained.

The leader must be aware of any personal and professional issues employees may have and make appropriate adjustments and allowances while ensuring the necessary work gets done to the highest quality.

Product Flexibility – Think of a restaurant owner who for years has offered dine-in only services and now has added takeout and delivery options for their customers due to the circumstances. Think of coaches and speakers who are used to in-person appointments and events and now must offer online options to their clients. It's this kind of flexibility that keeps a business open and operating instead of obsolete and out of business.

Customer Flexibility – Understand the reality that during times of economic crisis, typically reliable customers may not pay as quickly as they would under normal circumstances. The buying or renewal process may be delayed as well. You might offer reasonable flexibility in terms of payment options and deadlines. Flexibility also matters even in the best of times. It's the equivalent of always having a Plan B. Not having one can be fatal to the well-being of your business. Every leader should have a flexibility plan that can last for ninety days if necessary. When creating your plan, ask yourself the following questions:

- What happens if the business must shut down due to some unforeseen circumstance?
- What happens if we lose our best client?

- What happens if our products or services become second-rate or even obsolete? (Talk to the folks at IBM if you don't think this can happen.)
- What if we lose one or more of our key people?
- What happens if I as the leader become ill or incapacitated?
- What do we do if we have to expand our operations rapidly? Do we have a plan for rapid growth or expansion?

Ultimately, I'm an optimist at heart when it comes to difficult times. The bottom line is that a crystal-clear leader needs to exhibit flexibility in both good times and bad.

Questions and Exercises:

1. How have you as a leader had to be flexible throughout your business career?

2. Do you have a flexibility plan for your business? Are your people aware of it?

3. Write down three primary issues that could conceivably change the fundamental premise or equation for your business over the next six months. Once done, review and revise your flexibility plan.

CHAPTER TWENTY
Continuous Improvement

We humans have one distinct advantage over our fellow members of the animal kingdom. A few of them may be faster, stronger, and more instinctual, but none of them have the ability to improve their lot in life by themselves. Humans do. To prove my point, I have never met a doctor who is an elephant, a lawyer who is a giraffe, or a dentist who is a hippo.

There are so many stories out there about people who have come from nowhere and nothing to become great successes. One notable example is Dr. Ben Carson, who rose from the streets of Detroit to become a celebrated neurosurgeon and occupied the position of Secretary of Housing and Urban Development (HUD) with the Trump administration. Another example is Mike Lindell. If the name doesn't sound familiar, he's the "My Pillow" guy you see on TV every fifteen minutes or so. He kicked a drug, alcohol, and gambling habit and built one of the most successful companies in America. He makes a good pillow, by the way. Both of these gentlemen epitomize the characteristics of a crystal-clear leader.

A leader who wishes to achieve that same level of success, or achieve whatever their definition of success is, must always continue to improve. It takes a certain mindset for continuous improvement—you must keep the following in mind:

- I may be an expert, but I don't know everything there is to know.
- There is always someone out there who knows something I don't.
- In order to be at the top of my game as a leader of my company and a leader within my profession, I must continue to grow and develop my skills.

If you read the introduction to this book, you know I came into leadership training and then coaching from a very low point in my life. If you had told me three years ago I would be in the position I am now as a leadership coach, not to mention authoring my fourth book, I would have laughed at you.

However, I still wake up every morning hoping to learn something new. I've been trained and mentored by the top experts in the leadership training and coaching world, but I'm always looking for more. I continue to work with coaches in the academic area of coaching and even in the area of neuroscience. Learning is continuous for me. It should be for every leader, and this drive should be imparted to all the people in your company.

If you don't believe me, think of a few companies that used to be household names—IBM and Blackberry. IBM was literally the gold standard when it came to computers and technology. Any smart investor had IBM stock in their portfolio, and IBM computers were in every lab in the country. They thought they were untouchable, and thus, they never invested in improving what they already had in existence. They never believed in the idea of the personal computer or the laptop. When companies like Apple and Dell came along, IBM was caught flatfooted. By the time they realized the predicament they were in, they had lost so much market share that it was too late. Their golden goose was cooked.

Blackberry suffered the same fate. They began as a player in the area of cell phones and personal information devices. They had basically made the beeper a thing of the past, and all the top people in government carried a Blackberry. What happened?

Yup, Apple again. Their little invention known as the iPhone ran and operated much more simply and efficiently than the Blackberry. Then they turned around and invented something slightly larger called the iPad. The technology and operating system allowed them to provide all sorts of different apps and all the functions of the personal computer in the palm of your hand. I can only imagine the Blackberry is in the same resting place as the beeper.

Whether you like Apple and their products or not, they continue to invent and reinvent themselves regularly. The same principle applies to leadership. The leader who thinks they know all there is to know and believes they have reached the pinnacle of success is bound to fall off the mountain. Continued improvement is vital as a leader. This improvement also includes industry and leadership education. Think of it as oxygen for you and your company. Without that oxygen, you can be surpassed and made extinct in a hurry.

As the great pitcher and philosopher Satchel Paige once said, "Don't look back. Something might be gaining on you."

Questions and Exercises:

1. In what areas are you considered a leader in your industry? Why?

2. What is your company working on now to maintain its competitive advantage in the industry?

3. What are some of the trends happening in your industry that might change it over the next one to five years?

4. How can you as a leader improve your leadership abilities, your company's competitive edge, and its service delivery?

5. What can you do consistently each day to improve yourself as a personal and industry leader?

CHAPTER TWENTY-ONE

Hard Work and Preparation

So many things in life are beyond our control. From day to day, you can never completely predict what life may bring. The COVID-19 pandemic is the perfect example. Who in the world would have possibly believed a virus from across the world could bring the United States to a complete shutdown for months?

The only thing we as leaders can control is how we respond to our challenges and surroundings. One of the few things we know we can control is how hard we work. The harder we work, the greater our chances of success.

When I flew out to California to do my interview with Jack Canfield, we had a chance to spend some time together off camera. I asked him why he and others had extended themselves to me. I promise they don't (and can't) do that for everyone. His answer was, "You've worked incredibly hard and gone well above and beyond what anyone could have reasonably expected from you." Quite a compliment.

Look, we are all from a different place in life. Everyone has certain advantages and disadvantages. The great equalizer is hard work.

I can tell you flat out that hard work cannot be coached or taught. This is the one skill every crystal-clear leader must bring to the table themselves. I used to *think* I worked hard. I probably did too. With that said, though, I think my definition of hard work might have been a little off base.

As I began my study of leadership, I recognized my mistake. I had confused hard work with *productive* hard work. I've italicized the word *productive* for a reason. Productivity is a big key to crystal-clear success.

Here are some dos and don'ts for productive hard work:

DO

- Concentrate completely on your job while working.
- Set deadlines and stick to them. This includes training your employees to do this as well.
- Complete your tasks each day as scheduled. Prioritize the most important tasks by numbering them in order of their importance.
- Schedule downtime to keep yourself alert and refreshed. Stick to the schedule.
- Also schedule time to spend with family and friends, exercise, and enjoy leisure activities. Be *present* when you're doing these things.

DON'T

- Allow distractions to deter you from doing the work only the leader can and should do.
- Do the work others should be doing. Delegate accordingly.
- Work eighteen- to twenty-hour days. It's unhealthy, unproductive, and ridiculous.
- Burn yourself out.
- Work when you know you're too tired to be productive. It's more important to get some rest. The off hours will make the work hours more productive.

Along with hard work, the crystal-clear leader always needs to be prepared. To be ill-prepared as a leader is inexcusable; it's almost willful failure, and it sets an extremely poor example to the people you lead. That statement may sound harsh, but it's one-hundred percent the truth.

When I ran my former company, there were times when I didn't prepare to the level I should have, and I paid a steep price for it. When I began JTD Coaching, I made a vow that I would never be unprepared for any meeting, any phone call, any client, or anything else ever again. I am proud to say I have kept my vow without fail. It's one of the reasons I'm reaching new levels of success.

The National Basketball Association (NBA) legend Larry Bird of the Boston Celtics used to shoot one thousand free throws before every game. Hall of Fame Coach Bill Walsh of the San Francisco 49ers used to script the first twenty-five plays on offense and defense for every single game. Coach John Wooden kept notebook upon notebook of plays as well as the strengths, weaknesses, and tendencies of not only his own players but all the players in the team's conference. It's that kind of preparation that separates the legends from everyone else.

I have several standing meetings each week. They range from coaching sessions and meetings with my marketing team to sessions in which I'm coached myself. I take extensive notes on everything, and I always give myself forty-five minutes to an hour to review all the pertinent information before I begin the next session. I review my notes and then do what I call a clean-up. It allows me to reorganize my notes into a narrative I can read and review easily. I then bookmark everything, so I know exactly where I need to pick up next time.

Due to a more intense focus on hard work and preparation, the difference in results for me as a leader and the success of JTD Coaching has been amazing. Believe me, not every day goes smoothly, and there is no avoiding the inevitable hiccups that come with any and every business.

The major difference now is that I feel confident and comfortable with my ability to handle anything and everything that might happen. This is true even though I've actually had to manage more situations and deal with more people than I ever did in my previous twenty years in leadership, and that includes Disability Mentoring Day.

Preparation every day *for* each and every day has made all the difference.

Questions and Exercises:

1. Are you always as prepared as you should be for whatever may come up on a daily basis? What does that preparation look like?

2. What can you do to improve your preparation process?

3. Is your work productivity what it should be?

4. Are you taking care of yourself as a leader and as a human being? How do you keep yourself healthy and fresh to assure you are the best leader you can be every day?

CONCLUSION

Writing this book has been an amazing experience for me. During the writing process, I actually learned some new things!

That really is the idea behind the crystal-clear leadership concept—getting better, learning more, and achieving the happiness and success we all want and deserve on a personal and professional level.

The great gift of our country is that anyone can start from anywhere and succeed. And even if they fail as badly as I did, they can always start again and change the narrative. You only fail for good when you surrender and quit.

I came pretty close. I thought there was nothing left for me except the permanent stain of failure—personally and professionally. I was wrong. Thank God I didn't quit and miss out on the amazing, incredible opportunities that were in store for me. Crystal-clear leadership defines all I have learned from those opportunities.

This book has reached its end, but if you are interested in further study and/or individual and group coaching on the Eric Jackier Leadership System and the Crystal-Clear Leader, visit www.jtdcoaching.com and register for one of our many programs. I look forward to hearing from you and doing all I can to help you reach your leadership goals.

We will be introducing other crystal-clear leader tools as time goes on. The next book in the series will cover crystal-clear management. We will continue to expand as we move forward. I also welcome suggestions and ideas as everything develops.

No leader has all the answers—I'm no exception. I'm just an ordinary guy who was a failed leader and was given an extraordinary opportunity to successfully reinvent himself.

I hope you found, and will continue to find, this book helpful. The questions and exercises are meant to be worked on and used as often as needed. Change is inevitable, so the answers you come up with today may not be the ones you have in six months or a year from now.

Remember, leadership is a journey, and achieving leadership excellence is a journey within itself. You likely won't achieve everything all at once. Just keep plugging away each and every day and you will succeed.

At the end of the Brian Tracy Speaking Academy, he presented each participant with an individual gift. In my case, it was his amazing book *Maximum Achievement*. I was touched to find out later that it is his favorite book of all the ones he has written. On the front page, before the table of contents, he wrote the following:

To Eric,
You Can Do It!

I leave you with the same message.

ACKNOWLEDGEMENTS

First and foremost my family - Mom and Dad, Diane, Seth and Jamie
The Tobin Family
Mkada Beach who helped me start it all

My Professional Friends and Mentors:
Brian Tracy
Jack Canfield
Dr. David Krueger
Patty Aubery
My Coach and dear friend Ann Babiarz and her husband Michael
David Nield for his unique insights and great help throughout the entire journey

My wonderful team at JTD Coaching:
Gary Chappell
Michael Croteau
Jared Mast

Special thanks to Chris Sham, Frank Cipola, and Rachel Reclam for their many contributions and insights to JTD

The wonderful team at GracePoint Publishing for their help, support, and hand holding when I needed it.

Finally, to my readers, thank you for reading this book. I hope you find it helpful. I look forward to hearing from you.

ERIC JACKIER'S PROFESSIONAL AFFILIATIONS AND CERTIFICATIONS

Certifications

International Coach Federation - Certified Coach

Center for Executive Coaching - Certified Executive Coach

Coach Training Alliance - Certified Life Coach

Center for Executive Coaching - Master Certified Coach Trainer (pending)

The Canfield Training Group - Certified Success Principles™ Coach

John R. Wooden Pyramid of Success – Certified Coach

NeuroMentor® Institute for Peak Performance and Training - Certified Coach

Affiliations

Affiliated Partner—Brian Tracy International

Affiliate Partner—MentorPath Inc.

Coaching Partner—Train the Trainer (Jack Canfield)

Member of the International Coach Federation

Member of the World Business Executive Coaching Society (Europe)

ABOUT THE AUTHOR

Eric has had a long career in both the business and non profit sectors. He worked in broadcasting, sales, fund raising and education. Eric was the Chairman of the Disability Mentoring Day program in New York City from 2005-2014. The program helped thousands of people with disabilities explore and work in their chosen areas of career interests. Eric began JTD Coaching Inc. in 2019. He holds several certifications including the Jack Canfield Success Principles (Train the Trainer), The John R. Wooden Pyramid of Success Course, and is a Certified Coach with the NeuroMentor Institute of Peak Performance. He is also a member of the International Coach Federation and holds the title of Certified Executive Coach from the Center for Executive Coaching.

For more information on Eric and JTD Coaching please visit www.jtdcoaching.com

For more great books, please visit GracePoint Publishing online at www.gracepointpublishing.com